GUITARLELE

for Ukulele & Guitar players

by Terry Carter

UKE LIKE THE PROS

ISBN: 978 - 0 - 9826151 - 7 - 1

Copyright 2018

UKELIKETHEPROS.COM

Table of Contents

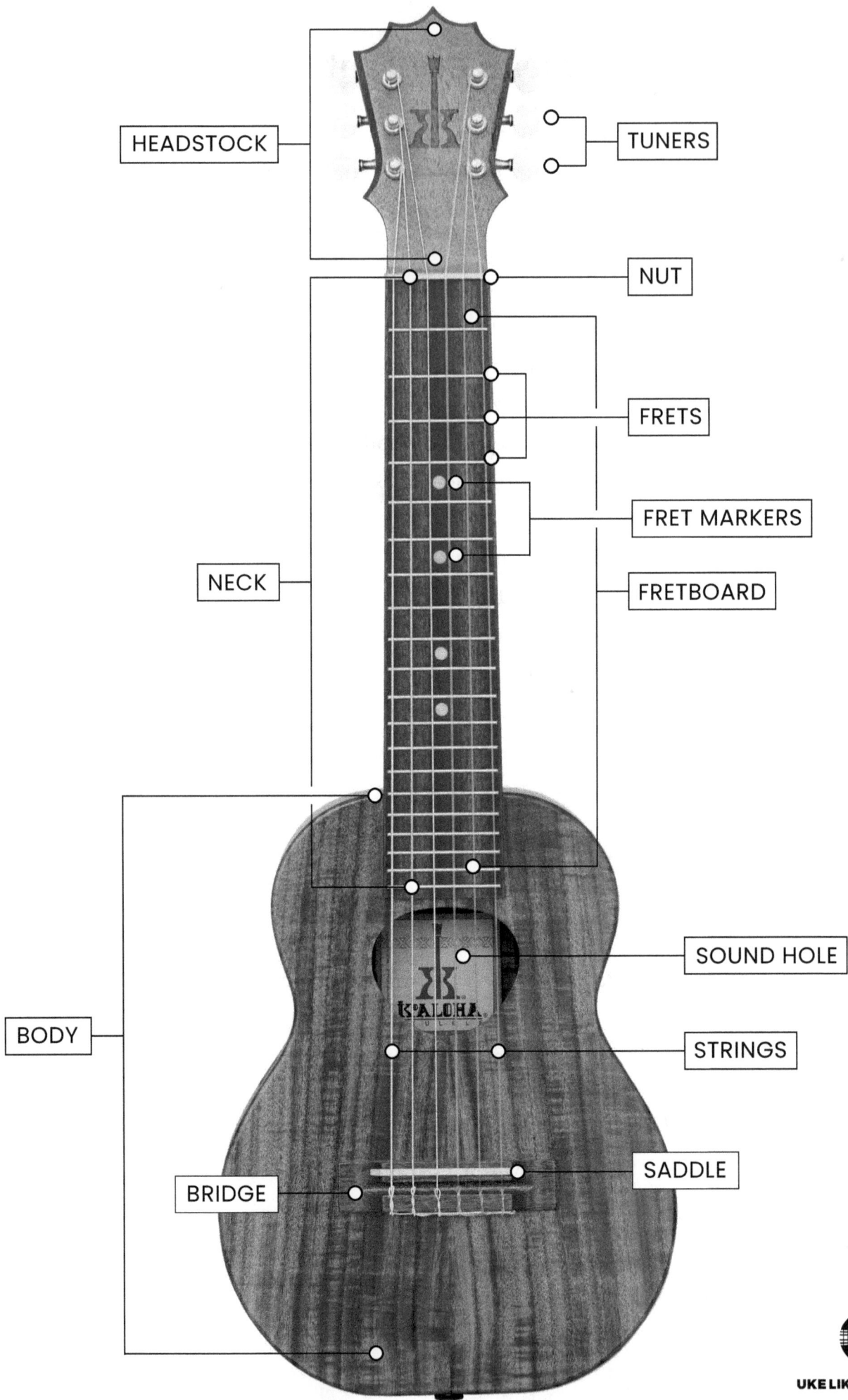

HEADSTOCK

TUNERS

NUT

FRETS

FRET MARKERS

NECK

FRETBOARD

BODY

SOUND HOLE

STRINGS

K°ALOHA

SADDLE

BRIDGE

A

UKE LIKE THE PROS.com

THE ESSENTIALS

It is important to learn and memorize these terms and symbols because they not only apply to Guitarlele but to all music.

Treble Clef or "G" Clef

Staff

Time Signature

Measure Numbers

Measure or Bar

Bar Line

End

Top Number:
How Many Beats Per Measure

♩= 120 — **Tempo Marks**
120 bpm (beats per minute)

Bottom Number:
What Kind of Note Gets the Beat

Common Time:
Same as 4/4 Time

Repeat Sign

Notes On The Staff: There are seven notes in music (A, B, C, D, E, F, G) and they move up and down alphabetically on the staff.

A B C D E F G A B C D E F G A B C D E F G

How To Remember The Notes:

Notes On The Lines

Notes in The Spaces

E (every)   G (good)   B (boy)   D (does)   F (fine)   F   A   C   E

HOW TO READ TAB

Tablature (TAB) is a form of music reading for Guitarlele that has been around for a long time. The TAB staff has 6 lines and each line represents a string on the Guitarlele. The number represents the fret you play on and are located on the string you play them on.

Strings
(Numbers & Letters)

1st String, O Fret (open)   6th String, 3rd Fret   1st String, 7th Fret

4th String, O Fret (open)   2nd String, 4th Fret

OPEN STRINGS ON THE GUITARLELE

These are the open string names for a guitarlele. When you play all the strings open on the guitarlele you get an Aminor11 chord.

Amin11

A   E   C   G   D   A

C

NOTES ON THE GUITARLELE NECK

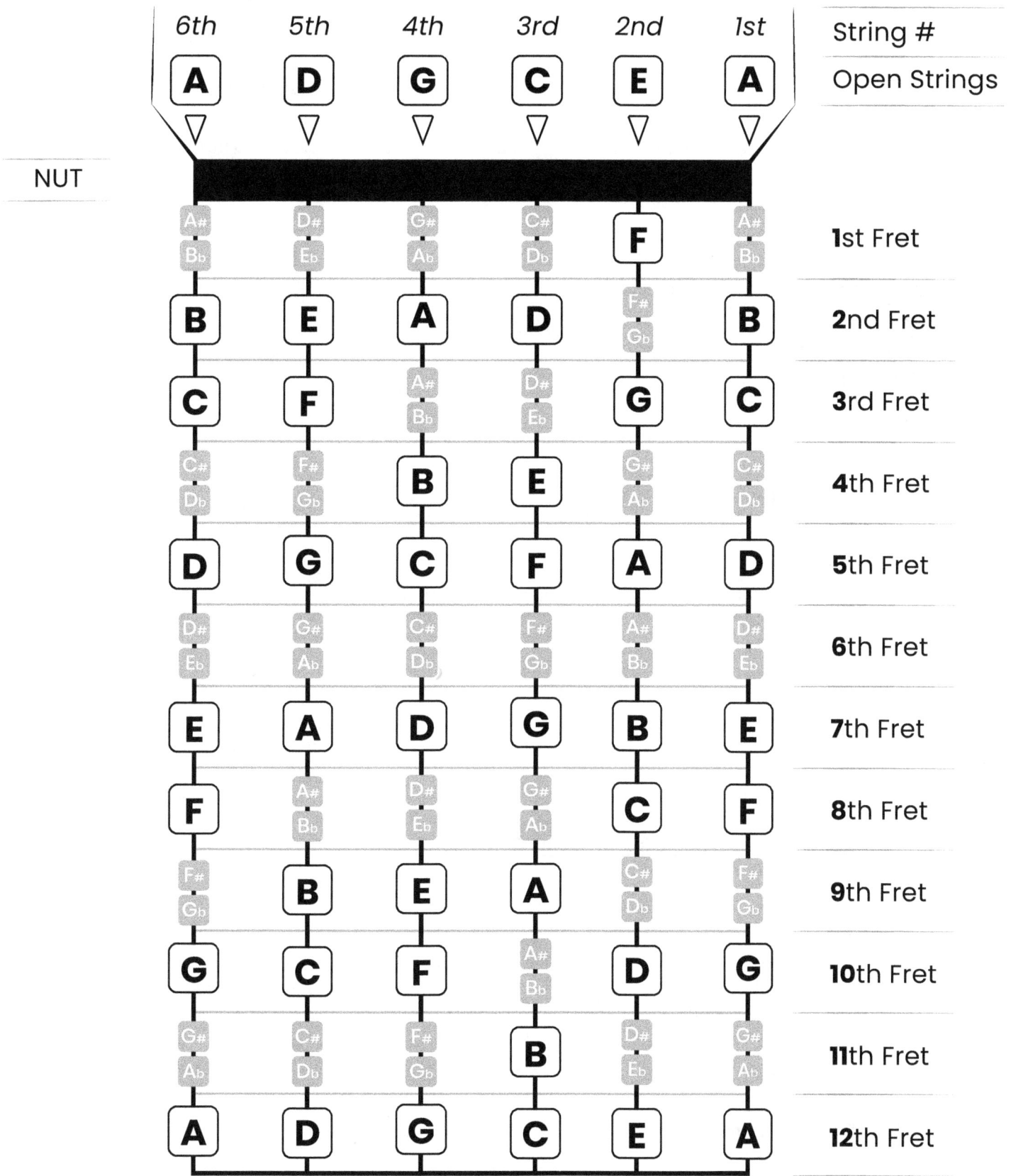

	6th	5th	4th	3rd	2nd	1st	
Open Strings	A	D	G	C	E	A	String # / Open Strings
NUT							
1st Fret	A#/Bb	D#/Eb	G#/Ab	C#/Db	F	A#/Bb	
2nd Fret	B	E	A	D	F#/Gb	B	
3rd Fret	C	F	A#/Bb	D#/Eb	G	C	
4th Fret	C#/Db	F#/Gb	B	E	G#/Ab	C#/Db	
5th Fret	D	G	C	F	A	D	
6th Fret	D#/Eb	G#/Ab	C#/Db	F#/Gb	A#/Bb	D#/Eb	
7th Fret	E	A	D	G	B	E	
8th Fret	F	A#/Bb	D#/Eb	G#/Ab	C	F	
9th Fret	F#/Gb	B	E	A	C#/Db	F#/Gb	
10th Fret	G	C	F	A#/Bb	D	G	
11th Fret	G#/Ab	C#/Db	F#/Gb	B	D#/Eb	G#/Ab	
12th Fret	A	D	G	C	E	A	

Notes repeat at 12th Fret

D

MUSIC SYMBOLS TO KNOW

A variety of symbols, articulations, repeats, hammer on's, pull off's, bends, and slides.

Fermata:
Hold note

Staccato:
Play note short

Accent:
Play note loud

Accented Staccato:
Play note
loud + short

Vibrato
Rapid "shaking"
of note

Arpeggiated Chord:
Play the notes in fast
succession from low
to high strings

Grace Note:
Fast embellishment
note played before
the main note

Mute:
"Muffle" sound of
strings either with
left or right hand

Down Stroke:
Pick string(s) with a
downward motion

Up Stroke:
Pick string(s) with
an upward motion

Tie:
Play first note but
do not play second
note that it is tied to

Ledger Lines:
Extend the staff
higher or lower.

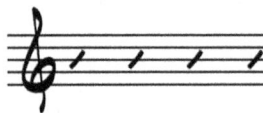

Slash Notation:
Repeat notes & rhythms
from previous measure

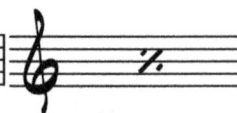

1 Bar Repeat:
Repeat notes &
rhythms from
previous measure

2 Bar Repeat:
Repeat notes & rhythms
from previous 2 measures

Repeat Sign:
(Beginning)

Repeat Sign:
(End)

1st Ending:
Play this part the
first time only

2nd Ending:
Play this part
the second time

(D.C. AL FINE) — *D.C.* (da capo) means go to the beginning of the tune and stop when you get to *Fine*

(D.C. AL CODA) — *D.C.* means go to the beginning of the tune and jump to *Coda* ⊕ when you see the sign ⊕

(D.S. AL FINE) — *D.S.* (dal segno) means go to the *Sign* 𝄋 and stop when you get to *Fine*

(D.S. AL CODA) — *D.S.* means go to the *Sign* 𝄋 And Jump to the *Coda* ⊕ when you see ⊕

SIM... — Play the same rhythm, strum pattern, or picking pattern as the previous measure

ETC... — Continue the same rhythm, strum pattern, or picking pattern as the previous measure

E

Hammer On:
Pick first note then hammer on to the next note without picking it.

Pull Off:
Pick first note then pull off to the next note without picking it.

Hammer On & Pull Off:
Pick first note, hammer on to the next note, and pull off to the last note all in one motion.

1/2 Step Bend:
Bend the first note a 1/2 step or 1 fret.

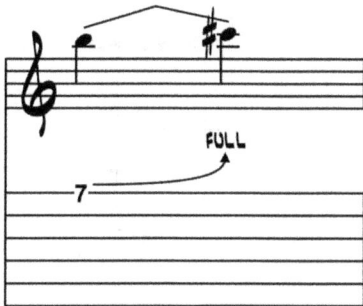

Whole Step Bend:
Bend the first note a whole step or 2 frets.

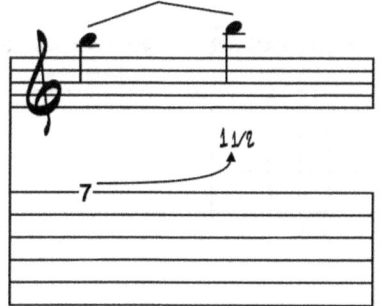

Step & 1/2 Bend:
Bend the first note 1 1/2 steps or 3 frets

Forward Slide:
Pick first note and slide up to higher note.

Backward Slide:
Pick first note and slide back to lower note.

Forward/Backward Slide:
Pick first note, slide up to next note and then slide back.

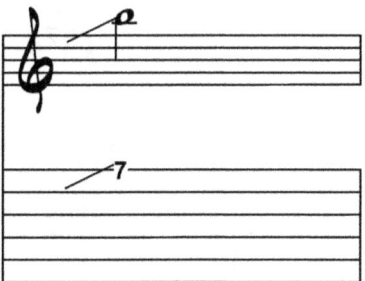

Slide Into Note:
Slide from 2-3 frets below note

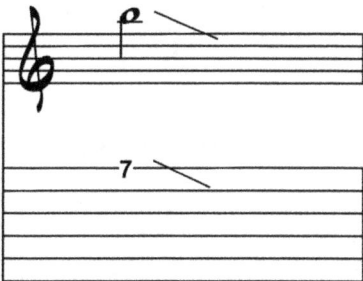

Slide Off Note:
Slide off 2-5 frets after note

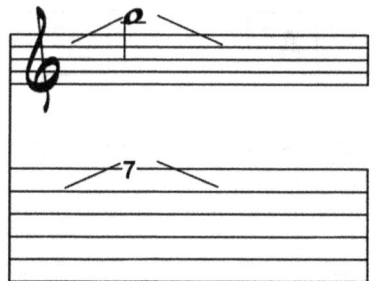

Slide Into Note then Slide Off Note

GUITARLELE CHORD CHART

These are some of the most widely used chords in all of music. Although there are more chords than what is listed, these chords represent the most widely used shapes. The string names (from high to low) are:

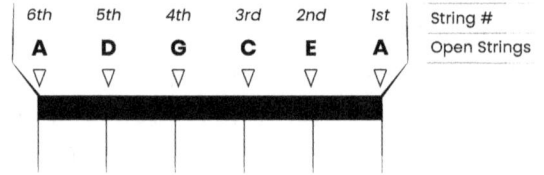

6th	5th	4th	3rd	2nd	1st	String #
A	D	G	C	E	A	Open Strings

MAJOR CHORDS

A — 2 3 1

B — 1 3 4 2 1 1

C — 2 1 3

D — 1 2 3

E — 1 2 3 4 1

F — 3 2 1

G — 1 3 2

MINOR CHORDS

A min — 2 3

B min — 1 3 4 1 1 1

C min — 1 3 4 1 1 1 — 3rd FRET

D min — 2 3 1

E min — 1 3 4 2 1

F min — 1 3 4 2 1 — 3rd FRET

G min — 2 3 1

7th CHORDS

A⁷ — 2 1

B⁷ — 1 3 1 2 1 1

C⁷ — 3 2 1

D⁷ — 2 3

E⁷ — 2 1 3 4

F⁷ — 2 1 3 1

G⁷ — 2 1 3

GUITARLELE CHORD CHART

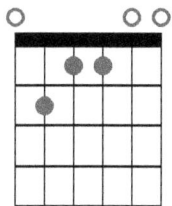 A maj7

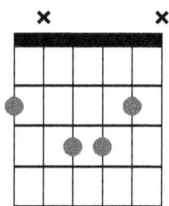 B maj7

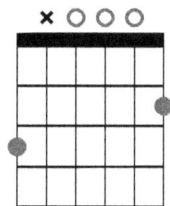 C maj7

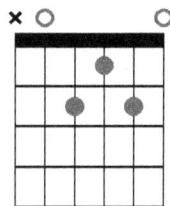 D maj7

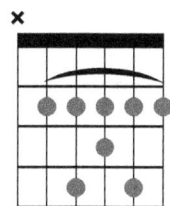 E maj7

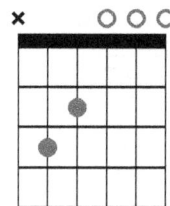 F maj7

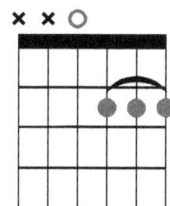 G maj7

MINOR 7th CHORDS

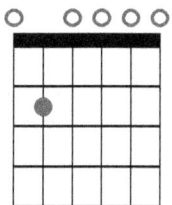 A min7

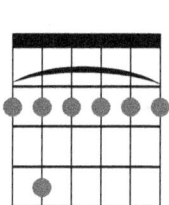 B min7

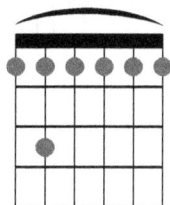 C min7

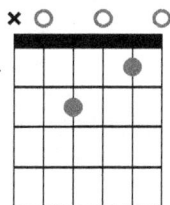 D min7

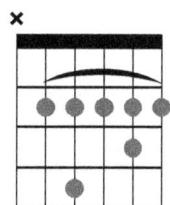 E min7

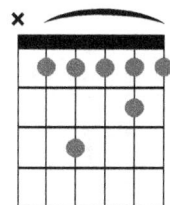 F min7

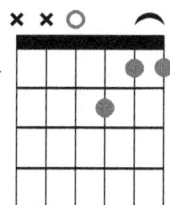 G min7

SUS + ADD CHORDS

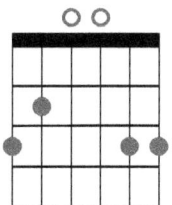 C

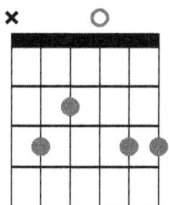 F add9

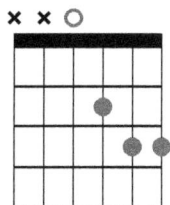 G sus4

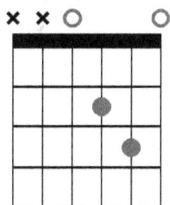 G sus2

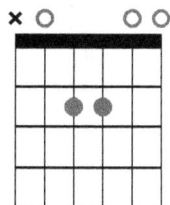 D sus2

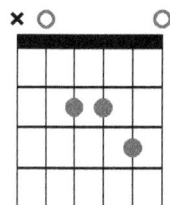 D sus4

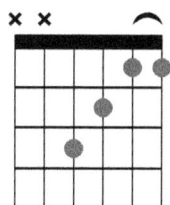 Bb

4 Finger C

Strumming Essentials

(Lesson 1)

This lesson will show you the "C" major chord and a down down-up strum pattern.

♩=106

C

1 + 2 + 3 + 4 +

1 2 3 4

Strumming Essentials

(Lesson 2)

This lesson adds the "Amin" chord and a half note on beat 3 to give you time to switch chords.

♩=106

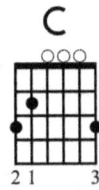 C   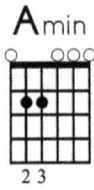 Amin   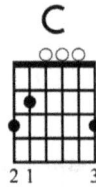 C   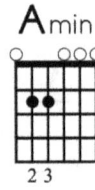 Amin    C

1 + 2 + 3 + 4 +

1 2 3 4

Strumming Essentials

(Lesson 3)

This lesson adds the "F" chord to the "C" & "Amin" chords and introduces a new rhythm.

♩=106

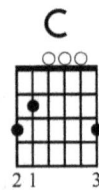 C   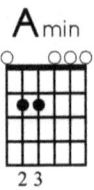 Amin   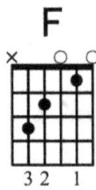 F   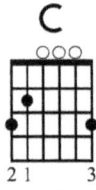 C

1 + 2 + 3 + 4 +

1 2 3 4

Strumming Essentials

(Lesson 4)

This lesson adds the "G" chord to the "C", "Amin", & "F" chords and introduces a new rhythm.

♩=106

Strumming Essentials

(Lesson 5)

This lesson adds the "Dmin" chord to the "C", "F", & "G" chords and introduces a new rhythm.

♩=106

Shine On

(In the style of Let it Be)

This chord progression is what is referred to as the I, V, vi, IV progression, aka the "Let It Be" progression. This is one of the most common chord progressions in music and can be heard on countless songs.

Blowin' Away

(In the style of Dust In The Wind)

This is a great song that uses "moving melodies" within chord shapes. All the chords in measures 1-4 are based on the "F" chord and all the chords in measures 5-8 are based off the "Dmin" chord.

Turning Point

(In the style of Good Riddance)

This progression using the Granddaddy Strum Pattern. For all the chords keep your
3rd & 4th fingers on the 1st & 2nd strings for the entire song.

No Hesitatin'

(In the style of Buddy Holly & Brown Eyed Girl)

The chords in this progression are some of the most important chords to know.

Gypsy Nights

This song has a Spanish flair to it that can be used to spice up any night,
D.C. al Fine means to go back to the beginning and play until the Fine.

Horizon's Sun

(In the style of House of The Rising Sun)

The time signature for this song is 6/8. The 6 means 6 beats per measure and the 8 means that the eighth note will get the beat. To put it simply 6/8 means 6 eighth notes per measure.

Dusty Roads Roll

This fingerstyle piece uses a forward roll with the *p* = thumb, *i* = index, *m* = middle, and *a* = ring. Each chord is played for 2 measures indicated by a one-bar repeat sign (⅟.). For each chord the bass note alternates between the root of the chord.

Meditatio #6 (excerpt)

by Terry Carter

This is a sample taken from the piece Fingerstyle Meditatio #6. It uses a backward roll,
which goes from the high strings to the low strings after you hit the bass note on beat 1.

Malagueña

A must know for all guitarlele players that is guranteed to be a crowd favorite.

Slidin'

Power Chord Song 01

This song uses two note power chords all on the 6th string. Make sure to slide
the entire chord shape up and down the neck when switching chords.

"Imagination is everything, it's the preview to life's coming attraction."

- Albert Einstein -

Wild Child

Power Chord Song 02

This standard rock progression uses the I chord (C), IV chord (F) and the V chord (G). All the chords are 3 finger power chords with roots on the 6th and 5th strings. This type of progression can be heard on songs like Wild Thing,, La Bamba, Beverly Hills and many more.

Classic 70's Rock

♩=84

"You build on failure. Use it as a stepping stone and close the door on the past. Don't try to forget the mistakes, but don't dwell on them."

- Johnny Cash -

Sweeping The Porch

(In the style of While My Guitar Gently Weeps)

One of the signature sounds of this progression are the slash chords (F/C & G7/B)
which give it a descending bass lines that goes from the D - C - B - Bb- A notes.

"You miss 100% of the shots you don't take"

- Wayne Gretzky -

Run Away

(In the style of Creep)

This song will challenge you with a contemporary sixteenth strum
pattern and the long intervals of playing bar chords.

♩=78

"I've had thousands of problems in my life most have never happened"

- Mark Twain -

Lemon Drops

(In the style of Somewhere Over The Rainbow)

An absolute classic that is an essential part of all guitarlele's repertoire.

Walking The Blues

One String Shuffle in D

Once you get down the phrase over the D7 chord, you will play the exact same phrase over the G7 and A7 chords but will be on different strings.

Wooly Bluecurls

(Blues Shuffle in the key of A)

This is a strumming Blues Shuffle. Pay attention to the mute (x) on beat 2 and the tie on the
"+ of beat 2." The last measure has a hip turnaround that you hear in many Blues classics.

Blues Shuffle

♩=128

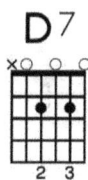

18

Tin Pan Alley

Blues Shuffle in D

This Blues shuffle is one of the most essential patterns you need to learn,
It uses a 2 string pattern and uses the I (D7), IV (G7), & V (A7) chords.

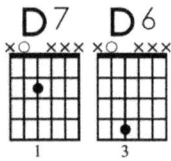
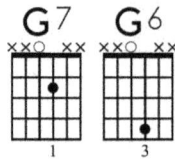
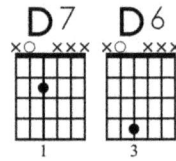

Swing ♪'s
♩=108

D7 D6   Cont.   G7 G6   Cont.   D7 D6   Cont.

```
1 + 2 + 3 + 4 +   Sim...
```

TAB:
```
  2-2-4-4-2-2-4-4    2-2-4-4-2-2-4-4    2-2-4-4-2-2-4-4        %
  0-0-0-0-0-0-0-0    0-0-0-0-0-0-0-0    0-0-0-0-0-0-0-0
```

Right Hand:
```
1 1 3 3 1 1 3 3   Sim...
```

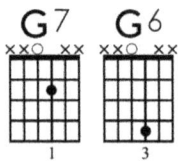
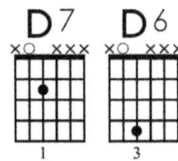

G7 G6   Cont.   D7 D6   Cont.

```
  2-2-4-4-2-2-4-4        %          2-2-4-4-2-2-4-4        %
  0-0-0-0-0-0-0-0                   0-0-0-0-0-0-0-0
```

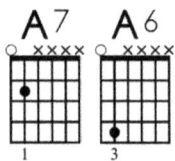
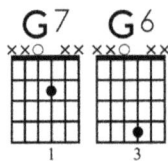
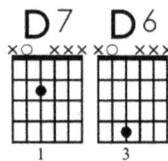
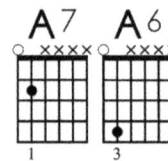

A7 A6   Cont.   G7 G6   Cont.   D7 D6   Cont.   A7 A6   Cont.   D7

```
                2-2-4-4-2-2-4-4    2-2-4-4-2-2-4-4    2-2-4-4-2-2-4-4        2
  2-2-4-4-2-2-4-4    0-0-0-0-0-0-0-0    0-0-0-0-0-0-0-0    0-0-0-0-0-0-0-0    0
  0-0-0-0-0-0-0-0
```

Smoke Stack Blues

Blues Shuffle in A

This Blues Shuffle is in the key of A and will require a power chord when we get to the E7 chord. This also has a traditional turnaround that uses triplets.

Car Insurance Blues

Straight Blues in A

This familiar sounding Blues lick was used in a commercial for a car insurance company, hence the name. The pattern is an arpeggio pattern based on the 1 - 3 - 5 - 6 - b7 for each chord.

Straight ♪'s

♩=142

Repeat the previous 2 measures

C7

Sim...

Counting: 1 + 2 + 3 + 4 + Sim...

```
T
A   |                           2—2   3—3—2—2
B   |         2—2—5—5                        5—5—2—2
    | 3—3
```

Right Hand: 2 2 1 1 4 4 1 1   2 2 1 1 4 4 1 1 Sim...

F7   C7

```
                        2—2   3—3—2—2
         2—2—5—5                  5—5—2—2                    2—2   3—3—2—2
3—3                                        2—2—5—5                     5—5—2—2
                                   3—3
```

G7   1. C7   G7

```
                  4—4   5—5—4—4
   4—4—7—7                   7—7—4—4
5—5                                      2—2—3—3—4—4  5—5—3—3—2—2
                                  3—3                           5—5
```

"You never want to fail because you didn't work hard enough"

- Arnold Schwarzeneger -

Backwood Blues

Chuck Berry Style Blues in C

This is the rhythm that help make Chuck Berry the Godfather of Rock & Roll.

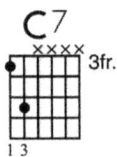
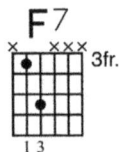
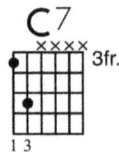
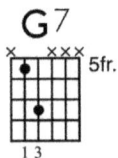
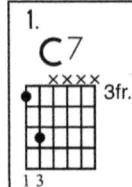

Straight ♪'s
♩=130

Sim...

"*Never guess who someone is just by looking at them,
you have no idea what they have gone through in life.*"

- Terry Carter -

I Hear The Train-A-Coming

(In the style of Folsom Prison Blues)

This is a country blues in the style of Johnny Cash, which is also called a "Train Beat".
It is in the key of A Major and the progression is only 8 bars long but it uses 16th notes
and an alternating root - 5th bass pattern on beats 1, 2, 3, & 4.

© Uke Like The Pros 2018

I Hear The Train-A-Coming pg. 2

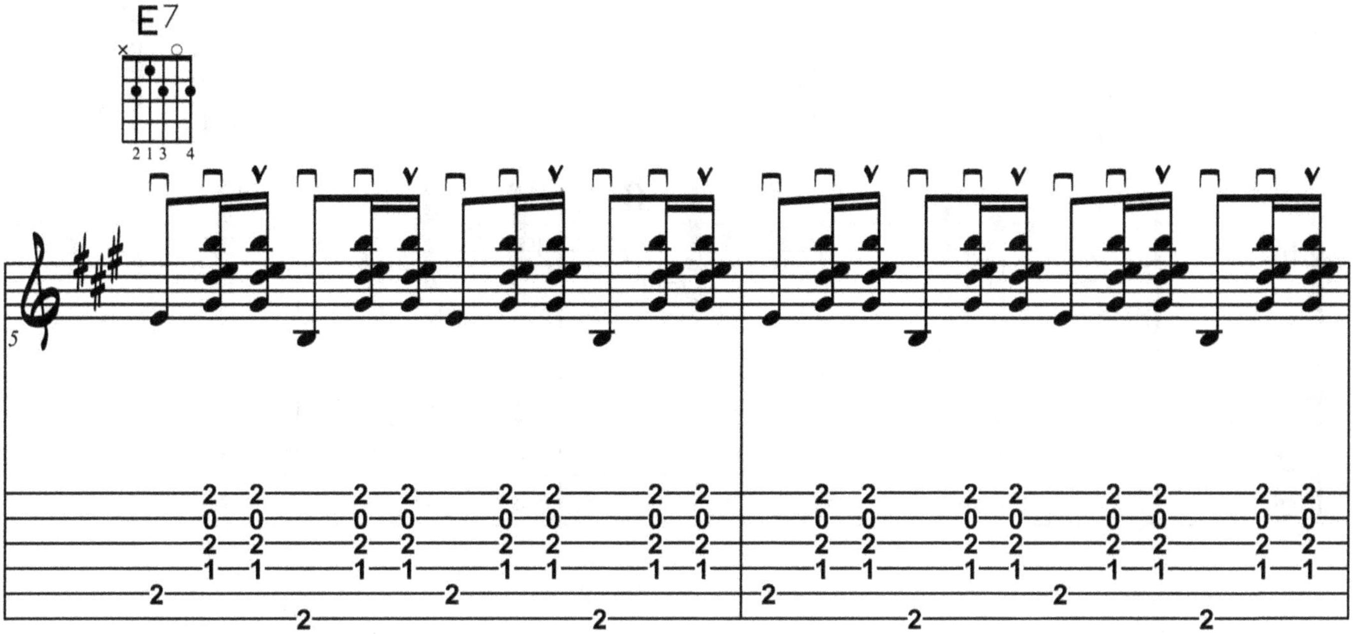

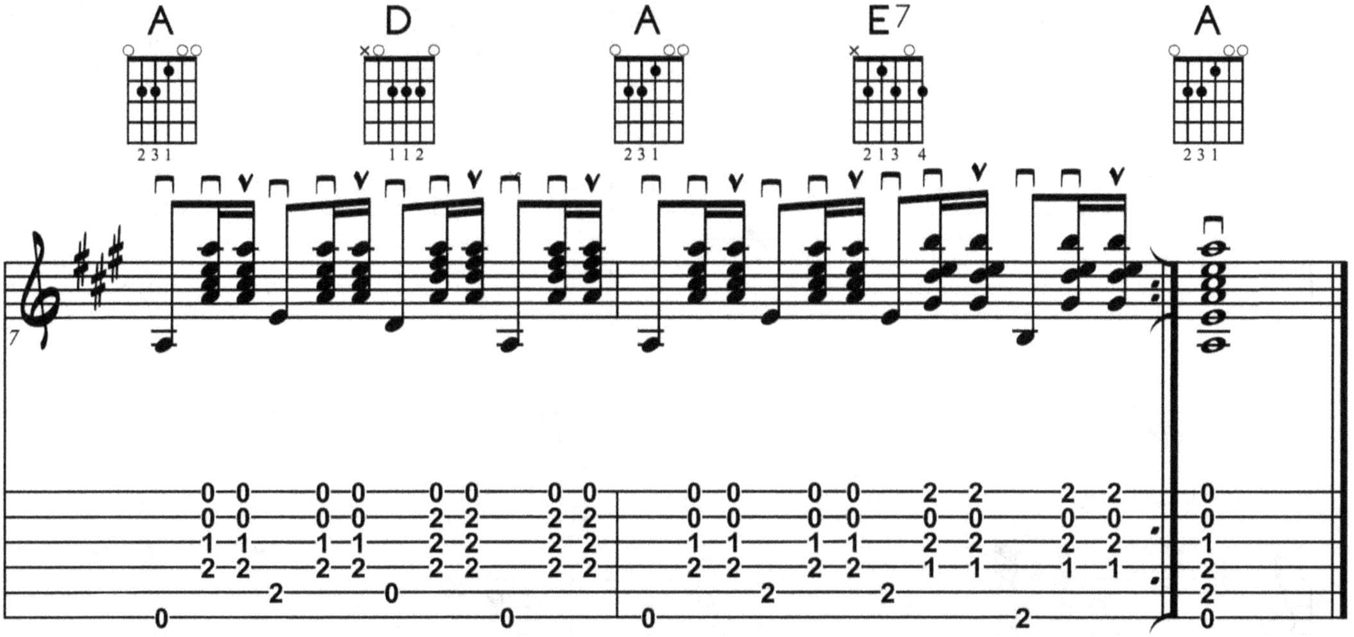

St. Charles Street Blues

This Jazz Blues is in the key of Bb and has a few more chords than traditional blues.

"Never half ass 2 things, whole ass one thing"

- Ron Swanson -
(Parks and Recreation)

A Major Scale

(Open Position)

This major scale uses 3 notes per string. Make sure to get this memorzied as soon as possible using the proper fingering.

♩=96

C Major Scale

(Closed Position)

This pattern is one of the most widely used major scales by guitarlele players. Once mastered it can easily be moved up and the the neck to adjust to the key that you are playing. Make sure to get this memorzied as soon as possible using the proper fingering.

A Minor Pentatonic Scale

(Open Position)

The Minor Pentatonic scales are one of the most important scales to know if you want to solo over a Blues or Rock song. It can be heard from artists like Led Zeppelin, B.B. King, John Mayer and countless others. This one is in the open position and works great over a song in the key of A

C Minor Pentatonic Scale

(Closed Position)

This minor pentatonic scale is referred to as the 'box' pattern. Once memorized it will be your best friend as you can use it over many songs and it is easy to transpose to different keys by sliding the shape up and down the neck.

D Minor Pentatonic Scale

(Open Position)

This minor pentatonic scale has the root on the open 5th string. This will sound great over a Blues in the key of D. Get it memorized and follow the proper fingerings.

F Minor Pentatonic Scale

(Closed Position)

This minor pentatonic scale is referred to as the 'box' pattern. Once memorized it will be your best friend as you can use it over many songs and it is easy to transpose to different keys by sliding the shape up and down the neck.

♩=96

Fingering: 1   4   1   3   1   3   2   4   1   4   1   4

```
T |------------------------|-----------------------|---3---6---3-----------|
A |-------------3---5------|---3---5---4---6--------|-----------------6-----|
B |---3---6----------------|-----------------------|-----------------------|
```

Fingering: 2   3   1   3   1   4   1   4   1   4   1

```
T |---4-------------------|-----------------------|-----------------------|
A |-------5---3---5-------|---3---6---3-----------|-------------------3---|
B |----------------------|-----------6---6---3---6|---3---6---------------|
```

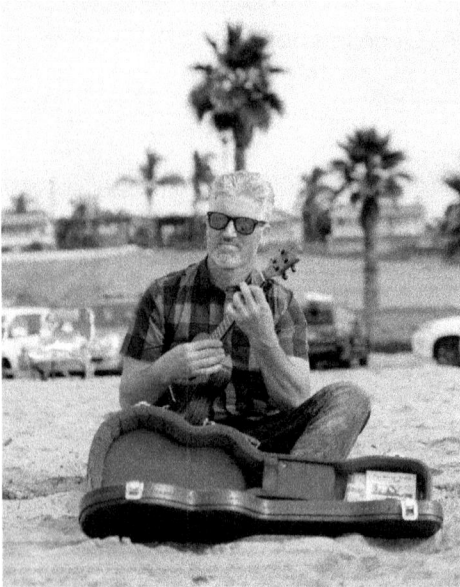

About the Author

Terry Carter is a San Diego-based ukulele and guitar player, surfer, educator, and creator of Uke Like The Pros. Terry has worked with Weezer, Josh Groban, Robbie Krieger (The Doors), 2 time Grammy winner composer Christopher Tin (*Calling All Dawns*), and the Los Angeles Philharmonic. Terry has written and produced tracks for commercials (Puma) and various television shows, including *Scorpion* (CBS), *Pit Bulls & Parolees* (Animal Planet), *Trippin' and Wildboyz* and *The Real World* (MTV). Terry received a Masters of Music in Studio/Jazz Guitar Performance from University of Southern California and a Bachelor of Music from San Diego State University, with an emphasis in Jazz Studies and Music Education.

Want to play better faster?

Join the growing community at www.UkeLikeThePros.com and get instant access to step-by-step video lessons, courses and improve your playing at a faster rate.

Other book from Uke Like The Pros

Ukulele Beginning
Music Reading

Master The Ukulele 1

Available on:

amazon

www.ingramcontent.com/pod-product-compliance
Lightning Source LLC
Chambersburg PA
CBHW062109090426
42741CB00015B/3373